The Holy Ground Around You

Reflective services for taking the church outside

Susan Sayers

kevin mayhew

kevin mayhew

First published in Great Britain in 2012 by Kevin Mayhew Ltd
Buxhall, Stowmarket, Suffolk IP14 3BW
Tel: +44 (0) 1449 737978 Fax: +44 (0) 1449 737834
E-mail: info@kevinmayhewltd.com

www.kevinmayhew.com

9 8 7 6 5 4 3 2 1 0

ISBN 978 1 84867 469 1
Catalogue No. 1501320

Cover design by Rob Mortonson
© Image used under licence from Shutterstock Inc.
Edited by Nicki Copeland
Typeset by Richard Weaver

Printed and bound in Great Britain

Contents

Foreword and thanks

There are books about wild swimming and wild food gathering, and this is a book about 'wild worship'. Not 'wild' in the sense of being 'out of control', but of being in touch with wild places in God's company. It is about getting outdoors under the sky in all weathers; getting our feet muddy; worshipping under the stars or lying flat and cloud watching. In the name of comfort, we have shut the natural world out of our worship; this book will get you out there in the amazing outdoors again! Holy ground is all around you.

The book contains short acts of worship for families, groups of friends, church groups, youth groups, pilgrimages, retreats and conferences. You can combine them with parish events such as summer fairs, carol singing, firework parties, picnics or family hikes. And once you get the idea, you can create your own services for your favourite wild worship venues.

I would like to thank my family, my church and my Franciscan friends for trying out these services and landscapes.

Why worship outside?

Our church buildings are a wonderful part of the gift handed down to us from those who have been worshipping God for many, many years before we were born. As we, in our turn, pray and worship faithfully in them, these special buildings become houses of prayer. The very buildings speak to visitors of God's love and peace and presence.

But it is important that we also worship in places where our souls and our feet touch base with the planet we are blessed to live on. Buildings, however beautiful, and our comfortable lifestyle, can anaesthetise us to the reality and weathering of our surroundings, unless we sometimes make the effort to dress appropriately and familiarise ourselves once again with the outdoors.

Standing out in God's creation refreshes us. It helps us recognise our place in the universe and reminds us that we are all part of this extraordinary miracle of love. As we allow God to lead us 'beside still waters', 'through the valley of the shadows', or 'in green pastures', we discover that God does indeed 'restore our soul' through attending to such places in worship.

The Celtic Christians knew this and breathed it. St Francis and St Clare found it when they swapped the life of luxury for its greater riches and freedom. Pilgrims discover it as they walk under the wide sky and feel the earth and rock beneath their feet.

Much of Scripture is told from the perspective of those who lived as nomads, learning the seasons and times of natural day, the stars and moonlight as well as the sun. The sounds of wind in the grass and trees, animals and birds calling, echoing thunder and flowing water were familiar, and the Scriptures spring to life in a fresh way when we hear them outside.

For too long, Christians have been unnoticed in their quiet, faithful praying. It is good and healthy that we do our praying sometimes where we might be seen by others, and without any other agenda. This is not mission in a structured way, but simply us delighting in God's presence. Strangely enough, it is often that candid, unembarrassed focusing on God which draws people, rather than our conscious attempts to draw them.

Yes, it can feel uncomfortable, standing out in the rain, taking off our shoes in a public place, or simply moving out of the familiar church building. But Jesus never spoke about being comfortable. And you will find that, once you take your courage in both hands and, quite literally, step out in faith, you will be amazed by the beauty of holiness in this simple act of worshipping in the open air.

All-weather suggestions

When we were kids, we would complain about having to go out in bad weather. My Dad used to say, 'There's no such thing as bad weather – only inappropriate clothing!' He loved going out in all weathers and I suppose I have inherited that. Thanks, Dad!

Make sure the group you are taking on these worship outings understands that there won't be any shelter; they will need waterproofs if it's raining and warm clothing if it's cold. I recommend that for wet weather everyone needs a waterproof hooded jacket, waterproof overtrousers and wellies. That way they will stay dry and happy instead of quickly becoming wet, cold and miserable. Umbrellas are useful but shouldn't be relied upon; if the wind is too strong, you will get wet. Far better to have an umbrella as an extra to your wet-weather kit.

People are often more ready to come prepared for sunshine, with head protection and sun cream. Light clothing that covers the body, arms and legs is excellent protection from the sun's radiation without the need for too much sun cream. It is important that everyone brings enough water to drink, too.

On rough terrain you will need a pair of strong trainers, shoes or hiking boots. For walking on the seabed where there may be sharp shells or broken glass, old trainers or jelly sandals are recommended. Wherever it is possible and safe, take off your shoes and feel the ground with your bare feet.

In cold weather, bear in mind that standing around outside will make you uncomfortably cold unless you dress warmly. It's no good dressing as you would for a quick breath of frosty air outside before scuttling into a warm shop or car. For these outings you need to be better protected, so wear a hat, gloves and scarf, a thick, windproof coat or jacket and warm trousers, socks and boots.

It's a good idea to bring a groundsheet for when you will be lying or sitting down, in case anyone has forgotten their waterproofs. Plastic sacks can also be used as groundsheets, or they can be cut to make an emergency waterproof jacket if necessary. Bring torches for night-time outings and plastic wallets for the service sheets to protect them from the weather.

Have a first-aid kit with you and carry out a risk assessment in advance to alert you to possible dangers and to prevent accidents as far as possible. Keep one copy of this with you and leave one copy with whoever is willing to act as the contact at base. Carry a phone and look after each other. Some of these wild worship outings are obviously more risky than others but, provided you have prepared everyone and are sensible, there is nothing dangerous about any of them. God's glorious, natural world is waiting for you. Go out and enjoy it!

Times and seasons

At dawn

Try this in different seasons of the year and in different places.
Face east. Have torches by which to read.
Gather while it is still dark so that you get a sense of waiting for the dawn.
Follow the service with breakfast together.

All night, while we rested and slept,
our planet earth has been turning. Still it turns, as we approach our hidden sun's light, already beginning to brighten our Eastern horizon.
Let us keep silence and stillness together,
honouring God our Maker, in the remaining darkness of night, as we wait for the sunrise of dawn.

Keep silence

Sense the planet on which you stand or sit turning to face the sun, rather than the sun rising over a flat earth.
Realise the roundness of the planet and us riding on its skin. Sense our smallness, and the great majesty of God's creation. Be attentive to the expectant waiting for dawn.

As the sun comes into view,
proclaim God's glory in a shout of praise:

Holy! Holy! Holy!
Holy! Holy! Holy!
Lord God almighty!
Lord God almighty!
Heaven and earth are full of your glory!
Heaven and earth are full of your glory!
Hosanna!
Hosanna!
Hosanna!
Hosanna!

Hosanna in the highest!
Hosanna in the highest!

We have now passed through the night
and the day is at hand! Blessed be God for ever!

Hymn *Morning has broken; This is the day* or *New every morning is the love.*

As we welcome this day
we honour the Father.
As we welcome this day
we honour the Son.
As we welcome this day
we honour the Spirit. We honour the blessed three, the blest Three in One.

Reading Genesis 1:1-5 (light is created) or Mark 16:1-7 (the resurrection).

This is the word of the Lord.
Thanks be to God.

Let us pray.
For those who have been longing for daylight,
Lord, hear our prayer.
For those who approach this day with fear and dread,
Lord, hear our prayer.
For those having to adjust to big changes in their lives,
Lord, hear our prayer.
For those to the north and south of us who share this dawn,
Lord, hear our prayer.

Our Father . . .

May the Lord our God bless us and keep us in the sunlight of his love.

At midday

You can be outside anywhere, at any time of year, and in any weather. Stand or sit in a circle, facing inwards. You might like to walk round in this circle and back to your place to start the worship. Singing as you walk is also an option.

Alleluia! The day is at its height!
Alleluia! The day is indeed at its brightest height! Planet earth has carried us here to the centre of this day's light.
Let us honour God, the Maker of the universe, as we stand together, centred, silent and still, in the centre of this day.

Keep silence

Notice where the sun's light is in relation to your circle.
Notice any shadows it casts.
Silent and still, in your spirit as well as your body, remember that you are on a spinning, orbiting planet, in the real presence of the Holy One. The permanent Spirit of God dwells with us in the temporary world we know.
God is here, watching us, familiar with us and full of love.

Holy God, you honour us with your presence,
and in your presence we rejoice.
You have brought us safely
to this moment in the day and to this moment in our lives.
You have been guiding us with your eye
and sometimes we have noticed, and sometimes we have not.
Once again, and with joy,
we rediscover the depth of your truth and love at the very heart of our being; at the very centre of the day.

Hymn *Be still for the presence of the Lord; Father we love you* or *Be still and know.*

Reading John 4:4-10; Mark 3:1-6 or Luke 23:44-46.

This is the word of the Lord.
Thanks be to God.

In the midst of our life and of this day, and conscious of the privilege of being alive, let us pray.
For those who struggle with heavy burdens in the heat of the day,
Lord of mercy, hear us.
For those for whom this day will be their last,
Lord of mercy, hear us.
For those who celebrate, full of joy today,
Lord of love, we thank you.
For those who are winning their battle with addiction,
Lord of love, we thank you.
For every word of kindness and every helping hand,
Lord of love, we thank you.

Our Father . . .

The rest of this day
to God we entrust it.
The work of this day
in God may we do it.
The life we are given
through God may we live it;
full and abundant and on into heaven.
Amen.

At dusk

Dusk is not a fixed time chronologically,
but describes that time between daylight and darkness.
Times of sunset will help you choose the best moment.
Any season or weather is good.
Have torches available for when it gets dark.
Face west.

Facing west towards the setting sun, we gather as others before us have gathered from ancient times, knowing that this day's light is coming to an end, and soon we will be in the darkness of night.

As the sun wakes others to a new day, so we lift our hearts and voices at this day's end, in thankfulness and praise.

Hymn *The day thou gavest, Lord, is ended; Abide with me* or *From the rising of the sun.*

As our planet turns, it hauls us away from the sun's light. Let us watch the beauty of the western evening sky and marvel at the majesty and mastery of God, the source of all beauty, both physical and spiritual.

Heaven and earth are full of your glory.
Hosanna in the highest!

Keep silence

Make yourself aware of the planet earth carrying you on its skin away from the sun, our local star.
Instead of seeing the sun setting, see the planet moving.
Imagine our sister planets also circling this same star.
Feel the peace of God's quiet presence
in the whole of time and place and beyond.

As the wonder of God's presence enfolds us in the fading light, we can proclaim, like Jacob, **'How awesome is this place! This is none other than the house of God, and this is the gate of heaven.'** (Genesis 28:17)

Reading Exodus 12:8-11; Isaiah 60:18-20 or Luke 24:25-35.

This is the word of the Lord.
Thanks be to God.

At this daylight's end, let us pray together.
Holy God, by day and by night may we be open to your love.

On our moving planet home, we have walked about today lit up by the sun since the dawn. As daylight fades into darkness, we bring you our thanks for all that has been good, our regrets for all that could have been more loving, and our forgiveness of any who have troubled us today.
Holy God, by day and by night may we be open to your love.

We pray for those who have been born today, and all for whom this day each year is special. We pray for those who have died today, those who have reached the end of their earthly life and are being born into the fullness of your presence. We pray especially for those who had no one to pray for them in the evening of their life. Through God's mercy and infinite compassion, may they be healed, forgiven and comforted.
Holy God, by day and by night may we be open to your love.

So often Jesus would choose this time to go off on his own to pray. May we live each moment in God's good company, and rest this night in God's peace and protection.
Holy God, by day and by night may we be open to your love.

Our Father . . .

May this evening be quietened with heaven's peace.
Amen.
May the good earth and all things living on it be in harmony with heaven.
Amen. Blessed be God for ever.

Under the stars

The less light pollution the better, but even moonlight renews our awareness of being space travellers in God's vast creation.
Bring torches but use them as little as possible.
Only the leader will need light during the worship.
Gather under the night sky.

We have gathered in the open air, under the wide sky, in the darkness of night, the time when space displays its distances, marked by the light of each star. Come, let us be still and worship God together in the wide space of all creation.

Keep silence

When I look at your heavens,
When I look at your heavens,
the work of your fingers,
the work of your fingers,
the moon and the stars that you have established;
the moon and the stars that you have established;
what are human beings that you are mindful of them?
what are human beings that you are mindful of them?
mortals that you care for them?
mortals that you care for them?

O Lord, our Sovereign,
O Lord, our Sovereign,
how majestic is your name in all the earth!
how majestic is your name in all the earth!
(From Psalm 8)

Glory to the Father, and to the Son, and to the Holy Spirit as it was in the beginning, is now and shall be for ever. Amen.

Our feet stand firm on the skin of our spinning planet earth.
Blessed be God for ever.
Our nearest star is hidden behind us, lighting the other side of the earth.
Blessed be God for ever.
God be praised in the circling dance of our planet family.
Blessed be God for ever.
The starlight we see is long since past, yet present to our eyes now.
Blessed be God for ever.
Our very bodies are made of ancient stardust.
Blessed be God for ever.
We join our song with the planets and stars of all creation.
Blessed be God for ever!

Reading — Genesis 15:4-6; Job 38:31-33 or Mark 13:35-37.

This is the word of the Lord.
Thanks be to God.

Let us pray for those who find it hard to sleep, for parents comforting fretful children, for those working in the emergency services and all on night shifts, and for all who are homeless with no shelter for the night.
Lord, in your mercy,
hear our prayer.

Let us pray for those who dread the darkness, for those using darkness as a cover for violence to others or themselves, and those for whom darkness is a blessed relief after an exhausting day.
Lord, in your mercy,
hear our prayer.

We pray for the forests and mountains, deserts, rivers and oceans, and all that is growing, hunting for food or being hunted this night.
Lord, in your mercy,
hear our prayer.

Let this night's rest refresh all who sleep and renew them in body and spirit. Defend us all from evil, within and without, and guard us from danger.
Lord, in your mercy,
hear our prayer.

Our Father . . .

God grant us a quiet night and peace on earth.
Amen.

In spring

Spring is a wonderful time to get outside to worship!
Gather where there is plenty of new growth around you, and maybe combine your worship time with planting seeds.

Walk round in a circle,
slowly and without speaking, and back to your place to begin.

The Lord is here.
His Spirit is with us!

We have reached that point in our earth-year's orbit of the sun when days lengthen and sap rises, roots are actively growing, and green shoots burst into the light of day.
We have reached that point in our earth-year's orbit of the sun when birds build nests, seeds sprout and days are warmer after the winter's cold.

In this, the springtime of the year,
let us rejoice in earth's awakening and in God's abundant provision.

Keep silence

Break from the circle and move around quietly, noticing the signs of spring and giving yourselves time to be filled with wonder at this yearly miracle of God's grace.
When the leader returns to the circle, make your way back as well.

Hymn *All creatures of our God and King; Praise, my soul, the King of heaven* or *We plough the fields and scatter* (which is a hymn for spring as well as for harvest).

Reading Matthew 13:31, 32 (the mustard seed).

This is the word of the Lord.
Thanks be to God.

With the springtime growth all around us, may we, too, be ready and willing to grow.
Lord, we offer you ourselves. Grow your kingdom in us so that the world may be blessed by your life fruiting in our lives, with love and compassion, faithfulness and truth.
With the hidden roots preparing to sustain the growing plants around us, may we, too, grow strong spiritual roots to sustain us on our journey of life.
Lord, give us the humility to welcome hidden growth, known only to you, and by living consciously in your presence may we become strongly rooted in your love.

If you are planting seeds as part of your worship, do that now, saying:

We plant these seeds in the name of the Father, who brings all things into being.
We plant these seeds in the name of the Son, who was willing to die in the flesh so that new life could be made available for all.
We plant these seeds in the name of the Spirit of God, who sustains and empowers us with all goodness and grace.
We plant these seeds in the name of the blessed Three in One, God of all Holiness.

Let us pray.

Keep silence and stillness

We thank you, good and gracious God, at this season of new growth and new life, for your wise and gentle care of us all, inhabitants of this earth.
For the precious gift of this moment, this day, this spring, this year,
we thank you, good and gracious God.

For the finely tuned and balanced universe, with all its life, life that is visible to us and life that is invisible to our eyes,
we thank you, good and gracious God.
For the diversity and richness of plant and animal life, seedtime and harvest, night and day, sun and rain,
we thank you, good and gracious God.

Our Father . . .

Heaven and earth are full of your glory.
Alleluia!

In summer

Gather preferably on a sunny day, in a garden, in a park or in the countryside.
If it's hot, sit in the shade, either in chairs or on the grass.
If possible, remove your shoes and worship barefoot.

In its yearly journey around our nearest star, planet earth tilts; and in this summer season this part of our planet is at its closest to the sun. The light and warmth give our planet life; the clouds and magnetic fields protect us; summer by summer the good earth provides all creatures with food and drink and the air we need to breathe.
Living within this miracle, let us take time to be thankful and recognise our blessings.
All these good gifts come from God, whose name is Love. God of Love, we give you thanks and praise.

Keep silence

If you are able, walk barefoot on the earth which gave you birth and whose gravity holds you safe.
Marvel at the summer season as part of the harmony and balance on our planet home.
Enjoy the leaves, flowers and seed heads, clouds and shadows.

O give thanks to the Lord, for he is good,
for his steadfast love endures for ever.
O give thanks to the God of gods,
for his steadfast love endures for ever.
O give thanks to the Lord of lords,
for his steadfast love endures for ever;
who alone does great wonders,
for his steadfast love endures for ever;

who by understanding made the heavens,
for his steadfast love endures for ever.
(Psalm 136:1-5)

Hymn *Be still and know; Be still for the presence of the Lord* or *Let all that is within me cry Holy.*

Reading Exodus 3:1-6; Luke 12:25-34 or Revelation 22:1-5.

This is the word of the Lord.
Thanks be to God.

Collect nine fruits, flowers or grasses and place them in the centre of the circle as the nine fruits of the Spirit are spoken.

Let us pray that fruitfulness may be the fragrance of our lives.
(Place the fruits/flowers as these spiritual fruits are listed)
Love. Joy. Peace. Patience. Kindness. Goodness. Faithfulness. Gentleness. Self-control.

Let Love blossom and fruit in us, so that we notice needs and respond with compassion.
Amen.
May our thankfulness and contentment release Joy in our own lives and the lives of others.
Amen.
May we long for Peace and become peacemakers, whatever the personal cost.
Amen.
Let Patience and Kindness soften our hearts towards those we find difficult, until all irritation melts away.
Amen.
May Goodness and Faithfulness be our priorities in all the choices we make so that our behaviour is Christlike.
Amen.
Let Gentleness, both to others and ourselves,

relax our urge for power and enable others to grow and fruit.
Amen.
May Self-control become an inner discipline, reminding us of our desire to be disciples of Jesus.
Amen.

Our Father . . .

God lets his sun shine and his rain fall on both the righteous and the unrighteous. So whenever the sunshine warms us,
it reminds us of God's love for everyone.

Whenever the good rain brings water to the earth,
it reminds us of God's love for everyone.

In this season of summer, may we delight in all God's blessings
and praise him joyfully with our fruitful lives.
Amen.

In autumn

If possible, gather where there are plenty of leaves on the trees, in their autumn colours. Meet during daylight. The actual time of day doesn't matter; the morning mistiness is beautiful and the afternoon sun on the coloured leaves is particularly glowing.

Begin with everyone moving around silently on their own. Move around to different places reverencing the earth as full of holiness, allowing God to show you the beauty of this autumn day in the whole of time and space. Summon everyone to the worship circle with a quiet gong or a wind chime.

When the gong or chime sounds, stand still in the presence of God as the leader gathers your reflections.

Keep silence

We stand on holy ground – earth dwellers on this autumn day of our earth-year. We are further from our sun star now, so that to us the sun looks lower in the sky. The summer days are shortening, and misty mornings remind us of the approaching cold of winter. Trees hang heavy with fruit. Spiders' webs shine with dew. The trees shut down their sap and leaves turn to gold and red and yellow before they fall.
Let us sing of God's faithfulness and ordered beauty.

Hymn *Great is thy faithfulness; Father, we love you* or *We plough the fields and scatter.*

The earth is the Lord's
and all that is in it,
the world,
and those who live in it. (Psalm 24:1)

Let us fear the Lord our God,
who gives the rain in its season, the autumn rain and the spring rain, and keeps for us the weeks appointed for the harvest. (Jeremiah 5:24)

Reading Genesis 8:22; Ruth 2:2-12 or John 4:31-38.

This is the word of the Lord.
Thanks be to God.

Lord of the harvest, under the shadow of whose wings we take refuge, we gather on this autumn day to thank you for your faithfulness and goodness, your generous love and mercy.
You have blessed us with the precious gift of life and given us this planet home in which to live out our days. Like the earth on which we live, may we too be fruitful. May we irrigate the barren, dry places that are starved of affection and justice by becoming channels of your refreshing and healing love.

Now, as we pray with longing for the heavenly to be earthed, so that justice and integrity, reconciliation and peace become a practical reality in our world, work on us to heal us so that we are better able to channel your love.
Take us as we are. Mend what is broken or damaged in us. Grow your harvest in us for the good of the world.

Keep silence

Stand or sit very still, and know yourself to be part of everything you see around you.
Let the autumn season teach you.
Open yourself to God as you keep in mind and heart your intention and longing to become the person God has in mind for you to be.

Let us pray as Jesus taught us, reflecting on the words as we say them slowly together:

Our Father . . .

As we enjoy the colour of these autumn days and glory in the richness of God's blessings, may we walk reverently on the earth and share its bounty with one another.
Thanks be to God, our Maker and Provider, now and all our days.
Amen.

In winter

Dress warmly and gather in a garden, churchyard or park,
in a local open space or on a walk.
Finish with hot drinks, either inside or,
if you are on a walk, from a flask.

We seek shelter from the winter cold. Standing here outside in the coldest season of the year is a kind of foolishness which helps to ground us in what is true and real.
Outside under the winter sky we stand together and praise the God of our making. Through harsh and gentle times God holds us.
Though in our homes we may shut the winter out, we know that in reality we inhabit a planet of heat and cold, summer and winter, light and darkness, sickness and health.
Blessed be God in the good earth and its seasons. Blessed be God through good and ill, weariness and rest, sorrow and joy.

Hymn *In the bleak mid-winter; Eternal Father strong to save* or *Will you come and follow me.*

As the bare trees, short days and cold weather surround us, we thank God for the warmth of our homes, for warm clothes and enough food. We know that without these benefits we would be hard pressed to survive the winter months.
We pray for those who find winter a harsh and challenging season.

We pray for those who are sleeping rough on our streets, those who cannot afford enough heating or light in their homes, the very old and the very young and all who are vulnerable to the cold.
Lord, we stand alongside them in their need, and offer ourselves to be part of your kingdom work on earth.

We pray for those in a spiritual or emotional winter, with bleakness and despair never far from the door. We pray for all who are hungry for peace of mind, companionship, acceptance or hope.
Lord, we stand alongside them in their need, and offer ourselves to be part of your kingdom work on earth.

We pray with thankfulness for all those who visit the housebound, the sick and the imprisoned, those who support the weak and encourage the fearful, those who feed the hungry and shelter the homeless.
Lord, we stand alongside them in their own need, and offer ourselves to be part of your kingdom work on earth.

Reading Psalm 130; Acts 27:33–28:2 or James 2:14-18.

This is the word of the Lord.
Thanks be to God.

Keep silence

Imagine yourself without a warm home to go to tonight, or food on the table.
Imagine being in a spiritual or emotional 'winter'.
Allow your imagination to help you stand alongside those in need and to pray for them.

Our Father . . .

In the season of winter, the cold and ice and snow enable many seeds to be prepared for growth in the spring. Hidden and asleep, the quiet enabling of new life goes on.
May we use this winter to rest our souls in humility and trustfulness within the shelter of the most high and holy God.

Whatever needs pruning or transforming in our lives,
let it be done in God's good time.

Whatever needs simplifying, or reshaping in our plans,
let it be done in God's good time.
As we celebrate the joyful earthing of heaven in the birth of Jesus,
so may Christ take up his dwelling place in our hearts and lives.
Amen.

Weather

In sunshine

The time of year isn't important, nor the time of day, nor the place; just the sunshine!
This worship might be part of an outdoor event such as a Fair, a party, a pilgrimage or a picnic.
Or it might simply be a celebration of a sunny day.
Gather in full sun or in the shade. Protect your heads and skin.

On this sunny day we want to worship God with thankful hearts and enjoy spending time in God's presence being warmed by the sun, our nearest star.
This is the day that the Lord has made;
let us rejoice and be glad in it. (Psalm 118:24)

Hymn *Give me joy in my heart; All things bright and beautiful* or *I watch the sunlight.*

Our circle reflects the shape of the sun and of the earth on which we live, from which our bodies come and to where our dust returns. The sun is our brother, without whose warmth and light there would be no life here at all. Let us praise God for the sun in the words of Saint Francis:
'May you be praised, O Lord, with all your creatures, especially Sir brother Sun, through whom you lighten the day for us. He is beautiful and radiant with great splendour. He signifies you, O Most High.
Praise and bless my Lord and give him thanks
and serve him with great humility.'
(From 'Canticle of the Creatures')

Our shadows cast by the sunlight, long at morning and evening, short at noon, mark for us the spin of our earth through the course of each day.

Between dawn and dusk we live and think and move and pray in the sun's shining light. And even at night the sun's reflected light shines on us in the darkness from our sister, the moon.
Be praised, my Lord, for sister moon and the stars.
Clear and precious and lovely, they are formed in heaven.
Praise and bless my Lord and give him thanks
and serve him with great humility.

Keep silence

You may like to walk around quietly, noticing the sunlight and shadows and thanking God for the sun that brings us life and energy and food.
Thank God, above all, for the sunshine of his love, shining on both the righteous and the unrighteous, gentle and full of kindness.
When the leader returns to the circle, take your place as well.

Like the sun, God's love warms us.
We are known to God and we are loved by God.

Reading

Psalm 121:5-8; Matthew 5:43-48 or Revelation 1:12-18.

This is the word of the Lord.
Thanks be to God.

Let us not take for granted the gifts of the sun and the earth,
but as good stewards let us share the resources and look after them well.
May we leave to our descendants
a legacy of blessing.

Our Father . . .

The Lord bless you and keep you;
the Lord make his face shine upon you and be gracious to you.
The Lord lift up the light of his countenance upon you and give you his peace.
My brothers and sisters, the Lord bless you.
Amen.

In rain

Put the words for the service in plastic bags or pouches, wear protective clothing and use umbrellas (as long as it is not too windy). The place and time of day are not important; just the rain!

We are going to praise God for the beauty of rain! With the rain falling all around us, instead of seeing it as bad news, let us welcome it as the blessing it really is!
Praise God for the blessing and beauty of the rain! Alleluia! Alleluia!

Keep silence

Walk around looking at the drops of rain, listen to the sound and smell the freshness. Notice the beauty.
Realise the miracle of rain watering the earth, bringing life and growth, gathering in streams, rivers and oceans.
Marvel at the ordered water cycle, with warm air carrying the moisture up into the clouds so rain can fall again. Above all, be thankful.
Make your way back to the circle.

Hymn *Peace is flowing like a river; Spirit of the living God* or *Rejoice in the Lord always.*

Sister water, falling as rain,
showing us again the abundance of God's love.
In each raindrop we can see the mystery of unity:
every stream and cloud and sea and ocean circling endlessly.
Sister water, so pure and clean,
showing us the generous cleansing and healing of God.
Sister water, so humble and useful,
when we stumble in our pride, we'll think of you.

In each raindrop we can see the mystery of unity:
every stream and cloud and sea and ocean circling endlessly.

Reading 1 Kings 18:41-46; Job 36:27-31 or John 4:10-13.

This is the word of the Lord.
Thanks be to God.

Sing to the Lord with thanksgiving;
make melody to our God on the lyre.
He covers the heavens with clouds, prepares rain for the earth,
makes grass grow on the hills. (Psalm 147:7-8)

You make springs gush forth in the valleys; they flow between the hills,
giving drink to every wild animal; the wild asses quench their thirst.
From your lofty abode you water the mountains;
the earth is satisfied with the fruit of your work.
(From Psalm 104)

Bless the Lord, O my soul, for his abundant goodness.
Alleluia!

Let us pray for places where there is little or no rain, and crops fail; where there is thirst and hunger.
Lord, we lift our hearts in prayer.
Let us pray for those who thirst for right, for peace, for justice, for truth.
Lord, we lift our hearts in prayer.
Let us pray for places where rain has caused flooding; for those whose lives and homes have been devastated.
Lord, we lift our hearts in prayer.
Let us pray with thankfulness for all whose lives are channels of God's peace, bringing life and blessing to others.
And make us channels of your peace.

Our Father . . .

May God's love and blessings rain down on the earth in plenty.
Amen.
May the water of life well up within us for abundant life which blesses those we meet each day.
Amen.
May God be praised in every moment and in all weathers.
Blessed be God for ever!
Amen.

In windy, stormy weather

Make sure you are dressed for the weather.
Choose a place that is safe but exciting.
Have the words in a plastic pouch or bag.
You may like to make this part of a kite-flying session.
Never fly a kite in a thunderstorm.

We have chosen to be outside in this wild and stormy weather so that we can worship God, the Lord of all weathers and all creation.
All glory to the living God of earth and heaven.

As children of earth, this created universe is home. The wild weather is like brother and sister to us. Through the Living Word we are all brought into being by our heavenly Father, the Great Holy One, God the Permanent, the Eternal Spirit.
God is Spirit and his worshippers must worship in spirit and in truth.
In humility, let us keep silence in this stormy weather and worship God in spirit and in truth.

Keep silence

Move around, sit or stand and feel the force of the weather.
Recognise the power of nature and our own vulnerability.
Now think spiritually of the great power of God and our frailty.
Worship the Reality of God and know your place of littleness
in the vast eternity of his Presence.

Let all that is in us cry Holy!
Holy! Holy! Holy! Is the Lord, the Almighty.
Heaven and earth are full of your glory!
Full of your glory, Holy God!

Yours, O Lord, are the greatness, the power, the glory, the victory and the majesty;
for all that is in the heavens and on the earth is yours; yours is the kingdom, O Lord, and you are exalted as head above all . . . And now, our God, we give thanks to you and praise your glorious name! (1 Chronicles 29:11, 13)

Hymn *Holy, holy, holy; Praise, my soul, the King of Heaven* or *O Lord my God.*

Reading Exodus 14:13, 14, 21, 22; Matthew 14:22-33 or Acts 2:1-6.

This is the word of the Lord.
Thanks be to God.

Let us pray for the wind of the Holy Spirit to blow afresh in our lives, to enliven our faith and to encourage us to go out and proclaim the good news of the kingdom of God.
Come, breath of God!
We pray for those who thirst for God's power and healing in their lives; for those who preach and teach others; for wisdom, humility and joy in the gospel of love.
Come, breath of God!
We pray for people, creatures and plants in danger from wind and storm, for fisherfolk on stormy seas, for those flying through stormy weather, and all whose homes or livelihoods are threatened by cyclones or tornados.
Come, breath of God!
We pray for the inward peace of God in all the storms of life – calm and reassuring, faithful and strong.
Come, breath of God!

Our Father . . .

Let us be blown in the wind of God's Spirit to the places and conversations and relationships that bless God's holy name.
Let it be so.

Let the Holy Spirit of God energise and empower
us for the work that blesses God's holy name.
Let it be so.
Let there be less of us and more of you, Lord God,
as we grow in your Spirit of love.
Amen. Let it be so!

In ice and snow

Make sure you are dressed appropriately for the weather.
Choose a safe place to gather.
You may like to make this worship part of a church walk, or gather on one of those days when a snowfall brings normal life to a standstill.
Any time of day is fine.
Use a triangle or bell to call people back to the circle after the time of silence.

Ice and snow transform the familiar landscape into a magical wonderland of soft shapes and glistening whiteness. So lightly and gently the snow settles. So quiet the world becomes.
Let snow and ice praise the Lord in their beauty and purity. With hushed voice and the untrodden perfection of freshly fallen snow, may the whisper of praise be heard. *(Whisper now)* **O Lord, our Maker, holy is your name!**

Keep silence

Look around at the white world and enjoy its fair beauty.
Notice patterns and shapes, separate snowflakes or icicles, black tree branches and trunks with the snow clinging to them.
Notice the sky and the clouds, shadows and sunlight or moonlight.
Notice the cold.
Allow God to draw your attention to what he would like to show you.
Make your way back to the circle when you hear the bell ring.

In the presence of such bright purity, let us come to the God of purity and holiness, who loves us. Let us confess our need of God's forgiveness and healing.

Have mercy on me, O God, according to your steadfast love;
according to your abundant mercy blot out my transgressions.
You desire truth in the inward being;
therefore teach me wisdom in my secret heart.
Purge me with hyssop, and I shall be clean;
wash me, and I shall be whiter than snow.
Create in me a clean heart, O God,
and put a new and right spirit within me.
(From Psalm 51)

The Lord hears the yearning of our hearts for purity.
May God's forgiveness transform us,
until our souls shine white as freshly driven snow.
Blessed are the pure in heart, for they will see God.

Hymn *I'm accepted; O worship the Lord* or *Such love.*

Reading Psalm 19:1-8; Luke 19:1-10 or James 3:17, 18.

This is the word of the Lord.
Thanks be to God.

Let us praise God for the delicate design of each fragile snowflake and the wonder of all creation, visible and invisible to our eyes.
God is good, all goodness and love.
We thank God for the mastery of this universe and our planet home with its seasons and delicate balance allowing life to thrive.
God is wise, all wisdom and faithfulness.
We long to honour God by the footprints we make during our life's journey here. May we tread every step carefully and with reverence.
God is humble, all humility and gentleness.

Let us pray for those in danger from the ice and snow.
Lord, hear our prayer.

For those in the emergency rescue services and their rescue operations.
Lord, hear our prayer.
For any who feel spiritually or emotionally cut off, frozen or lost.
Lord, hear our prayer.

Our Father . . .

From this white cold we shout our praise
and bless your name for ever:
Alleluia! God most holy! Alleluia!
God most high!
Praises ring from us your people, under the wide and winter sky.

Places

In the churchyard

Gather where you can see the church from the outside.
The time of day, season and weather are not important.
You may wish to make this part of a dedication festival or thanksgiving.
It is a good way to pray for the church and its life and mission.
If possible, pray barefoot.
Ring the church bell to call people back to the circle after the time of silence.

Welcome to this holy ground, in the churchyard and under the sky.
The ground beneath our feet, the air around us, close to one another and in the presence of God, we stand and worship. Blessed be God for ever!

Our church building, so often our shelter from the weather and the storms of life, is dear to us. Let us touch its walls and pray for God's blessing on the church we love.

Keep silence

Spread yourselves around the church walls wherever you can, placing hands on them in silent love and longing for God's will to be done in this building and this church community.
Allow the Spirit of God to guide you in your thoughts and prayers.
When the church bell rings, make your way back to the circle.

Our love for this church has drawn us to pray for the building and the church community. Our hands have touched the stones. And the reality is that God is doing just the same at every moment.

This church we love is loved and cherished by the God we worship there. To him all hearts are open and from him no secrets are hidden. To God, each living stone is precious and important, chosen and called.
Through years and generations, many have entered this church to pray and have left refreshed in spirit, strengthened and inspired.
We thank you, Father, Son and Holy Spirit, for all whose faithful lives have grown God's kingdom here.

Hymn *We love the place, O Lord; A new commandment* or *Be still for the presence of the Lord.*

Unless the Lord builds the house,
those who build it labour in vain.
Unless the Lord guards the city,
the guard keeps watch in vain. (Psalm 127:1)

Reading Matthew 5:13-16; John 15:1-8 or John 17:13-23.

This is the word of the Lord.
Thanks be to God.

Let us pray together for the church, that it may truly be a sign of God's kingdom, shining with holiness and love.
We dedicate ourselves afresh to your service, Lord God.
Let us pray for clear guidance, for open hearts to notice God's prompting and courage to act in obedience and humility.
We dedicate ourselves as your disciples, Lord God.
Let us pray for all who enter here, that they may find God's welcome in the welcome of God's church.
We dedicate ourselves as living stones, built into a living temple to your glory, Lord God.

Let us pray for the mission of this church, that through our outreach others may discover the truth about God and the abundant life that only God can give.
We dedicate ourselves to be available and ready for action, Lord God.

Our Father . . .

Let us circle the church with God's blessing.

Walk as much as possible around the outside of the church, singing as you go either *We are marching; O when the saints* or *Seek ye first the kingdom of God* as a blessing on the church.

Live the rest of the day consciously in the company of Jesus.

Under a tree

Before churches were built, worship often took place beneath a tree, as it still does in many parts of the world.
Choose your tree.
It may be in a garden or in a park, near the church; it may be a tree you are walking to on a mini pilgrimage.
Gather when there are still leaves on the tree.
Stand around the tree, barefoot if possible.

Under this tree we gather to worship the living God, Father, Son and Holy Spirit.
All praise to God our creator, redeemer, sustainer.
As part of God's creation, and in God's name, we honour and reverence
all ground and the ground on which we stand, the arching sky and these clouds, all trees and this tree, all creatures and one another here.
From this tree and from our feet in all directions stretches the rest of the planet, and the universe,
full of God's glory and love.

Keep silence

Unless the group is too big, stand sideways to the tree and each rest one hand on its trunk so that you are like the spokes of a wheel from its centre.
Look up into its branches and see how it has grown, twisting its way upwards. Notice the texture, shapes and colours of the bark and leaves.
Notice the shelter the tree provides for birds and insects.
In this one tree, honour and delight in God's remarkable creation.

For the grace and balance of the universe we share,
we thank you, holy God.
For the legacy of this great tree with its gifts of shade, fresh air and locked carbon,
we praise you, holy God.
For our own gift of life, and the gift of this day, and the gift we can be to the world,
we glorify you, holy God.

Reading Psalm 1:1-3; Matthew 13:31, 32 or Revelation 22:1, 2.

This is the word of the Lord.
Thanks be to God.

Hymn *All things bright and beautiful; Give thanks* or *For the beauty of the earth.*

We pray for the earth, that we may learn in humility how to look after it well and responsibly while we live and breathe on it.
Let your will be respected and accomplished on earth, like it is in heaven.
We pray for a better understanding of the value of trees and forests, and against the greed that leads to their destruction.
Let your will be accomplished in our own choices and spending, lifestyles and self-discipline.
We pray for the places already affected by global warming, and for the will and heart to act and help, and to recognise our excesses.
Let your will soak deep into our consciousness and galvanise us into joyful action.
May we rediscover the earthed and simple ways of living,
the earthed and generous ways of giving,
the joy of rooting, growing, fruiting
in the good earth of God's love.

Our Father . . .

Link hands around the tree and bless one another with God's blessing:

May the grace of our Lord Jesus Christ
and the love of God
and the fellowship of the Holy Spirit
be with us all
evermore.
Amen.

On the beach

Gather where you can look out over the water.
Stand or sit on the beach, barefoot if possible.
The time of day and season are not important – whatever suits you.
You may want to make this part of a beach party, or a baptism.
Hold some sand in your hands.

Though the mountains may fall and the hills turn to dust,
God's word will never fail. Blessed be the eternal God for ever.
Look at the sand we are holding. So many grains of sand held in the palms of our hands, and all on a journey from different places and ancient times, since long before there were any hands at all.
Stardust, molten rock, erupting volcano, ancient mountain, glacier debris, river washed, wave ground to this beach and this day and our hands.
We too are on a journey,
through time and space, between birth and death.
Storms may come and the road may be rough; we may lose our way altogether; mountain tops may be eroded to dust and rocks may be ground to sand,
and yet always there, in the stillness where past and future mingle together, rests the ever-present, unchanging God who cradles our living in his hand.

Keep silence

Walk around on the beach.
Notice the sounds, the smell and how it feels.
Under the sky, sense the vast and the very small.

Watch the waves pounding the stones and shells,
or the mud flats waiting.
Let the sand flow through your fingers and toes.
Enjoy solids so small they act like water.
Move back to the group in silence.

'To see a world in a grain of sand
and a heaven in a wild flower,
hold infinity in the palm of your hand,
and eternity in an hour.'
(From 'Songs of Innocence', William Blake)

Poised in the presence of both earth and heaven, let us sing out our praise and thanksgiving to the God of eternity.

Hymn *One more step; Immortal, invisible* or *I danced in the morning.*

Reading Psalm 102:25-27; John 14:1-7
or Hebrews 2:10-12.

This is the word of the Lord.
Thanks be to God.

We pray for this world of ours, its shifting tectonic plates, its warming and cooling climates, its magnetic protective fields driven from the great heart of it; for everything that thrives on the skin of it and the waters that cover so much of it.
Holy and eternal God, we worship you alone.
We pray for the mountain streams and crashing waterfalls, the widening rivers flowing out into the seas and oceans, for the moon-driven tides covering and uncovering the marshes and mudflats in the rhythm of ebb and flow.
Holy and eternal God, we worship you alone.
We pray for the towering cliffs and rocky ledges on windswept islands, for tropical beaches with coconut palms, for thriving docks and cities and harbours, for all the earth's great coastlines dipping into the sea.

Holy and eternal God, we worship you alone.

Our Father . . .

Where water meets land we have met with you,
Lord God.
You are with us in all the change and rhythm of our lives.
With sand and sea we sing our thanks and praise.
In joy and sorrow, in want and plenty, in time and in eternity,
in days and seasons, and in all weathers,
may your holy name be praised.
Amen.

In forest or woodland

Try making pilgrimage from your church
to a woodland or a forest, or make this worship a part of a family or church picnic.
The country, season and time of day are up to you.
Gather under the canopy of the trees. Check for ants' nests!
Bring a windchime or make a birdcall to gather people after the silence.

Let us lay down our own noises and agendas and listen to the forest around us, sheltering us, quietly growing.
Even the trees, and everything that lives here, are our brothers and sisters, for we are all part of God's beautiful creation.

Keep silence

Find a place on your own to be still.
Listen to the sounds of the forest.
Notice the other creatures for whom this place is home.
Smell the forest; touch and look at the textures, colours and shapes, the daylight and shadows, the earth and leaves under your feet.
Quietly make your way back to the circle.

Here in the forest we are like guests, visiting the living home of all we have met in our time of stillness. Here we are reminded that we are guests on the planet and in this moment of its history.
Fools rush in where angels fear to tread. Keep us humble and respectful as we live out our earth-days on our way to heaven.
Let us sing quietly in the beauty of this place, and reverence the God of earth and heaven.

Hymn *Be still for the presence of the Lord; Let all mortal flesh keep silence* or *To be in your presence.*

Holy God, your presence and peace surround us.
Be still, and know that I am God.
The living, growing forest is like the living, growing kingdom of God.
Be still, and know that I am God.
The birds of the air, the insects and the squirrels find food and shelter in the branches and fruits and abundance of leaves.
Be still, and know that I am God.

Reading Genesis 1:9-13; 1 Chronicles 16:29-34 or Ezekiel 47:7-12.

This is the word of the Lord.
Thanks be to God.

Among the trees in the quiet beauty of the forest, let us pray for peace.
Peace as a place of inner calm and contentment in hearts and lives that are stressed.
Peace of mind in those who are fearful.
Peace as the deep assurance that we are known, accepted and loved.
Peace of gentle simplicity which comes from a thankful heart.
Peace as laying down the urge to dominate, and taking up the joy of mutual cooperation.
Peace as giving up long-held bitterness, and forgiving instead.
Peace as accepting what cannot be changed and counting our blessings.
Peace as praying for blessings on those we find difficult to get on with.
Peace as sharing what we have.
Blessed are the peacemakers,
for they will be called the children of God.
(Matthew 5:9)

Our Father . . .

Beware of false prophets, who come to you in sheep's clothing but inwardly are ravenous wolves.
You will know them by their fruits.
Are grapes gathered from thorns, or figs from thistles?
In the same way, every good tree bears good fruit, but the bad tree bears bad fruit. Thus you will know them by their fruits.
(Matthew 7:15-17, 20)
Go and bear fruit,
fruit that will last. (John 15:6)
Amen.

On a mountain or hill

Any high ground where there is a view will be suitable – even the top of a multi-storey car park! Combine the worship with a picnic and some kite-flying, or a hike.
Gather at a suitable place.
Wear appropriate clothing for the weather and terrain.
Carry out a risk assessment in advance to ensure safety.

Mountains and hills have always been holy places, where heaven and earth feel close:
the climb, the view and new understanding of geography, the sense of being somehow 'set apart'.
Lord of earth and heaven,
on this high place we come to worship you.
Blessed be God, the Holy One. Alleluia!

Hymn *Praise, my soul, the King of heaven*; *Holy, holy, holy* or *Peruvian Gloria.*

Let us still ourselves and open our hearts and minds to the holy presence of the eternal God, who was there at the birth of this mountain and every mountain and has watched over us on our journey from birth to this moment and this place.

Keep silence

If possible, take off your shoes and feel the ground under your feet.
Sit or stand looking out over the view.
Look up at the great sky above you, over the lower ground and into the distance around you.
Know the reality – that God, who is Spirit, is here in person, all around us.
Let your own spirit be open and receptive to the loving presence of God.

My God and my all!
My God and my all!
Your gracious, loving presence fills us with joy and peace.
Lord God, you are lovely. You are good, all good, and we worship you.
Holy God, you are the source of all goodness, all holiness, all truth and all that is, both the visible and the invisible, the measured and the immeasurable.
Your love reaches to the heavens and fills the depths of the earth.
Holy, holy, holy, Lord God Almighty. Heaven and earth are full of your glory!

Reading

Exodus 19:16-19 and 20:18-21;
1 Kings 19:11-13 or Matthew 5:1-12.

This is the word of the Lord.
Thanks be to God.

Who shall ascend the hill of the Lord? And who shall stand in his holy place?
Those who have clean hands and pure hearts, who do not lift up their souls to what is false, and do not swear deceitfully.
They will receive blessing from the Lord, and vindication from the God of their salvation.
Such is the company of those who seek him, who seek the face of the God of Jacob.
(Psalm 24:3-6)

Let us pray that God will forgive us our sins and heal us with his love.
In your presence, O God of purity and love, we recognise our need of your forgiveness. We confess to you the unkindness, selfishness, dishonesty and meanness of our thoughts, words and deeds. Purify and heal us by your Spirit. Wash us clean and give us courage to live as you would have us live.

May God, who loves us, and who hears the authentic cry of our hearts, wash away our sin and clothe us in integrity and generous love.
Amen. Thank you, Lord God, for saving us and setting us free.

Our Father . . .

May we go on our way from here rejoicing.
As we leave the heights of this place, may we bring down with us the inner peace of God.
For God is here and will be always with us.
Way, Truth, and Life. Alleluia!
Amen!

In a cave or ravine

Gather in a place that is safe and ensure that the group is safely led and equipped.
The journey is an integral part of the worship.
Pray together as you set out, and know yourselves to be called on pilgrimage as you travel to this place.

Let us thank God for bringing us safely to this time and this place.
Father God, you have watched over us and we thank you for your guidance both for the body and for the soul. We come to seek your face, your will and your kingdom.
As we worship God here in the rock of this place,
may we be renewed, refreshed and challenged by God's will for us.

Hymn *Will you come and follow me; Great is thy faithfulness* or *O Jesus I have promised.*

Reading 1 Samuel 24:1-12; 1 Kings 19:1-11 or John 11:32-44.

This is the word of the Lord.
Thanks be to God.

As we, too, stand in the shelter of the rock, and our hands touch the strength of the rock around us, may we be attentive to the quiet voice of the living God.

Keep silence

Touch the rock and feel its shape and texture.
In the darkness or shadow, listen carefully.
Listen to the earth sounds and also to the quiet presence of God, who knows you by name and is ready to guide your life and work with you for great blessing.

Be attentive to your heart's longing, any hopes or regrets, and the deep desire to serve God and seek his face.

God does not always meet us in the places of comfort, but the rocky places of challenge.
In this wild place we journeyed to find, God meets us as we really are.
Come, Spirit, come. Take charge of my mind.
Show me the darkness that you find.
Help us to trust you, even with our shame, till we freely acknowledge where we are to blame.

Let us pray with longing for the kingdom of God and his righteousness.
Your kingdom, O Lord, let it come in fullness on the earth! Your will, O Lord, let it happen on earth like it happens in heaven!
On the valleys and hills, the mountains and caves,
let your kingdom come!
In the dark, rocky places of desolation and in the depths of guilt and despair,
let your kingdom come!
In the hearts of all who seek out your face,
let your kingdom come!
In the crumbled illusions and broken promises of our world,
let your kingdom come!
In the valiant struggle for peace, justice and hope,
let your kingdom come!

Our Father . . .

The Lord is my shepherd, I shall not want.
He makes me lie down in green pastures; he leads me beside still waters;
he restores my soul. He leads me in right paths for his name's sake.
Even though I walk through the darkest valley, I fear no evil; for you are with me; your rod and your staff – they comfort me.

You prepare a table before me in the presence of my enemies; you anoint my head with oil; my cup overflows.
Surely goodness and mercy shall follow me all the days of my life, and I shall dwell in the house of the Lord my whole life long.
Amen. (Psalm 23)

Beside a river, stream or canal

Pay careful attention to safety and ensure that everyone in the group is safe at all times.
Gather in a place where you overlook the water and sit down together.
This worship may be part of a walk and picnic, or a pilgrimage.

The Lord, our God, has led us to gather here beside the water.
As we lay our burdens down, may we rejoice in the refreshment God loves to give his children.
May we collect ourselves in God's good presence and listen to his love.
We are here to worship and adore you, gracious God, and we thank you for the comfort of your presence with us, here and in every moment.

Keep silence

Be still. Relax and be at peace in God's presence.
Enjoy God's creation all around you.
Look at the sky and clouds, flying birds and insects.
Look at the glint and sparkle of flowing water and any fish swimming.
Look at any grasses, trees or flowers growing beside the water.
Feel the moving air on your face and your own quiet breathing.
Let the stillness enable you to sense the peace of God.

Be still
and know that I am God.
Within and without us.
Below and above us.

At our right and at our left.
Before and behind us.
God encircles us and fills us with the presence of his peace.
Glory to the living God, Father, Son and Holy Spirit.

Hymn *The King of Love my shepherd is; As the deer pants for the water* or *Peace is flowing like a river.*

The wilderness and the dry land shall be glad; the desert shall rejoice and blossom.
For waters will break forth in the wilderness, and streams in the desert;
the burning sand shall become a pool, and the thirsty ground springs of water;
the haunt of jackals shall become a swamp, the grass shall become reeds and rushes.
And the ransomed of the Lord shall return, and come to Zion with singing; everlasting joy shall be upon their heads;
they shall obtain joy and gladness, and sorrow and sighing shall flee away. (From Isaiah 35)

Reading 2 Kings 5:11-14; John 7:37, 38 or Revelation 22:1, 2.

This is the word of the Lord.
Thanks be to God.

Flowing, living water reminds us of the spiritual living water which Jesus offers us, abundant and free.
May we be soaked in the abundant watering of the Holy Spirit of God. May it be to us renewing, refreshing and cleansing.
When our wells run dry and we find ourselves trusting in our own strength,
flood our souls afresh with the living water which brings us to life.

Our Father . . .

Let us pray for the people of God in every land and situation,
for the river of God to flow deep and wide throughout the whole church.
Let it give new depth to faltering faith,
fresh delight in God's love,
full cleansing from sin,
gentle soothing of all that is aching,
drink to the thirsty,
refreshment to the weary.
Jesus, Water of Life,
may the Church wade deep in the glorious joy and freedom of your love.
Amen.

At the end of a jetty or pier

The idea of being here is to look out over the sea and be standing right above the water, almost like being on a boat.
You can be on a boat if you prefer!
Address safety issues thoroughly.
The time and season are flexible.
You may want to include the walk (or ride) to the end of the pier as an introduction to the worship.

We gather here in the name of the Father, the maker of sea and sky.
We gather here in the name of the Son, who walked on water to reach his anxious friends, and calmed the raging sea.
We gather here in the name of the Holy Spirit, who brooded over the waters at the beginning and whose calm presence holds all things in being.
Holy God, we worship and adore you in this place of beauty, above the sea and under the sky.

Hymn *This world you have made; Wide, wide as the ocean* or *Lead us, heavenly Father, lead us.*

Through the seas and oceans we are connected with all the coastlines of the world.
Flowing between the different shores, these waters lace us all together.
We are all brothers and sisters of the same heavenly Father,
living together on our blue and green planet, white with clouds and ice caps.
Praise God from whom all blessings flow! Praise him, all creatures here below.
Praise him above, ye heavenly host! Praise Father, Son and Holy Ghost.

Keep silence

Stand still in the breeze and the smell of the sea.
Study the clouds above and the waves below.
Look far into the distance and sense the truth of our rounded planet.
Think of the water flowing between coasts all over the world.
Think of God's love flowing and connecting, reconciling and buoyant.

Life emerged first from within water.
Blessed be God for the miracle of life.
Water surrounds each baby on the growth journey to birth.
Blessed be God for the miracle of life.

Reading Genesis 1:20-23; Mark 6:45-51 or John 21:1-14.

This is the word of the Lord.
Thanks be to God.

Let us pray for God's blessing on the seas and oceans and all that lives in them.
May the seas and oceans of earth be healthy and clean, respected and cared for, reverenced as part of God's creation.
Let us pray for those who make a living from the sea.
May sensible and wise decisions be made to protect the ocean life and to promote sustainable ways of fishing. Let there be less greed and more respect for this precious resource.
Let us pray with thankfulness for all the gifts the seas and oceans give us.
We give you thanks and praise for the diversity and beauty of marine life and the ocean beds; for the privilege of standing to wonder and worship; for the challenges facing us, that they may not scare us but become opportunities to address the needs of future generations.

Our Father . . .

Let the curl of the breaking waves calm your spirit and give you peace.
Amen.
Let the seabird's call and the salt-sprayed air refresh you in body and soul.
Amen.
May God's great love, wider and deeper than the sea, enfold you.
Amen.

In the grounds of a castle or historic building

This gathering is for the sense of history, so ruins are fine.
You may want to combine this worship with a community day out, or go somewhere local.
Choose a safe and good place to gather and, if possible, remove shoes so that you are barefoot on the grass.

Welcome to this particular moment which we all share. We are all alive on this same day even though we were born on different days in different circuits of the sun. Welcome to the present!
We have all have travelled through time and space to meet in this circle. In the name and presence of Jesus we welcome one another as we gather to worship the God of time and eternity.

Greet one another, sharing the peace of God.

Back through the generations our families can be traced, our shared genetic make-up verified, our family features and habits emerging afresh in every new family member.
The buildings around us testify to other lives and choices, other hopes and dreams, in the chain of human beings stretching back through time;
the wealthy and protected, the struggling poor,
the indolent and useful, optimists and pessimists,
faithful and forgiving,
arrogant and cruel.

As for mortals, their days are like grass; they flourish like a flower of the field;
for the wind blows over it, and it is gone, and its place knows it no more.

But the steadfast love of the Lord is from everlasting to everlasting on those who fear him,
and his righteousness to children's children.
(Psalm 103:15-17)

Keep silence

Look at the walls built long ago, and touch them if you can.
Imagine the people and animals who would have lived and worked here.
Imagine people's sadnesses and celebrations, worries and prayers.
Recognise that you, too, are mortal and live on the earth only for a time.
Be thankful for everything in life which perhaps you take for granted.
Refresh your appreciation of daily miracles
and even of what can be learned from the difficult times.
Know yourself to be part of the human race, not only across the present world but also in the unfolding of time.

Lord of eternity, from this place and time on the earth we give you thanks and praise
for the privilege of life and all its blessings and lessons.
We thank you for our families and our ancestors, through whom we are alive today.
We thank you for lives well lived, for courageous decisions known only to you,
for faithful prayer and perseverance in times of trouble,
for open hearts to one another and to you.
We commend them all to your unfailing, healing love and your presence in heaven.

Hymn *I heard the voice of Jesus say*; *Love divine* or *It came upon the midnight clear*.

Reading Luke 12:32-34; John 17:20-26 or Romans 8:31-39.

This is the word of the Lord.
Thanks be to God.

Our Father . . .

Praise be to the God and Father of our Lord Jesus Christ, the Father of compassion and the God of all comfort, who comforts us in all our troubles, so we can comfort those in any trouble with the comfort we ourselves have received from God.
All praise and thanks to God. Amen.

In a park or garden

We gather here to celebrate the beauty of creation and meditate on the garden of Eden in Scripture. Probably spring or summer is best, and fine weather, but provided you are clothed adequately, any weather is fine!

'Now the Lord God had planted a garden in the east, in Eden, and there he put the man he had formed.
And the Lord God made all kinds of trees grow out of the ground – trees that were pleasing to the eye and good for food.
In the middle of the garden were the tree of life
and the tree of the knowledge of good and evil.'
(Genesis 2:8, 9, NIV)

We have gathered in this garden to worship the Lord God of all creation.
The life and growth surrounding us proclaims the glory of God.
We marvel at the intricate beauty of each flower and seed, each leaf and branch.
How beautiful is the garden of this world in which we live and move. It tells of the power and gentleness, care and harmony of God, our Maker and Sustainer.

Keep silence

Think of God taking you by the hand and leading you around the garden, showing you what he loves and enjoys.
Walk quietly and slowly with your hand in God's hand.
Be attentive and wonder at what you are shown, as if this is the first time you have seen it.
And that is true in a sense – this is the first time you have seen this place in this moment.
Reverence it.

'Then the man and his wife heard the sound of the Lord God as he was walking in the garden in the cool of the day.' (Genesis 3:8, NIV)
In the still quietness we have discovered your Presence among us, Lord God, walking here in the garden with us today.
We thank you for walking with us, for taking us by the hand and leading us.
May we deepen our friendship with you as we walk increasingly in your company, content with your leading and your will for us.
May the garden of our soul be beautiful with herbs and flowers of thankfulness, small bright kindnesses, slow-growing shrubs of patience and perseverance;
with orchards of fruiting goodness, gentleness and honesty; water lilies in clear pools of contrition and repentance, surrounded by the sweet-smelling roses full of the joy of sins forgiven.

Hymn *Morning has broken*; *Be still and know* or *Father, we love you*.

Reading Genesis 1:11-13; Isaiah 58:6-11 or John 19:38–20:18.

This is the word of the Lord.
Thanks be to God.

As the different varieties of plants and creatures have developed and unfolded over time, so may our souls be gradually transformed by God's guidance and love.
My God and my all!
Jesus said, 'I am the true vine, and my Father is the vinegrower. Abide in me as I abide in you. I am the vine, you are the branches.'
(John 15:1, 4, 5)
My God and my all!

The earth is the Lord's and all that is in it. You give us the honour and responsibility of looking after the earth.
My God and my all!

Our Father . . .

May God's loving kindness take root in our lives and grow.
Amen.
May God's glory awake in us a wholehearted thankfulness.
Amen.
May the landscape of our being become the garden of God's love.
Amen.

By a lake, reservoir or pond

You may wish to combine this with a nature walk and picnic.
Gather in a safe place where you have a good view of the water.
The season and time of day are up to you.
You may wish to bring binoculars and a reference book.
Wear clothing suitable for the weather.

The Lord is my shepherd, I shall not want.
He makes me lie down in green pastures;
he leads me beside still waters;
he restores my soul. (Psalm 23:1, 2)
We have been led here, beside these still waters,
so that our souls may be refreshed and restored.
Let us take time to unburden ourselves of all that stresses and wearies us, and allow God to give us the gift of tranquillity and peace in this place of beauty.

Keep silence

Spend quality time simply enjoying the lake, its residents and visitors.
Being still will enable you to notice more.
Let the natural world teach your attentive heart about God.
Enjoy the beauty you notice with your senses, and praise God for it all.
This can be for a few minutes or for an extended time of an hour or so if you like.

Thank you, Lord God, for leading us beside still waters;
for giving us time to see more carefully and to value what we see.

We thank you for the birds and insects, their diligence and grace;
for the water's surface, reflective and calm.
We thank you for eyes to see with and minds to name;
for brightness and shadowy depth, for the scatter of water drops and ripples in widening rings.
He leads me beside still waters.
He restores my soul.

Hymn *The Lord's my shepherd; Seek ye first* or *This world you have made.*

As the water reflects the light, so let us settle to reflect on the word of God.

Reading John 14:23-27; Romans 12:9-21 or 2 Corinthians 3:16-18 and 4:16-18.

This is the word of the Lord.
Thanks be to God.

Let us pray that hearts and minds all over the world may faithfully reflect the love and goodness of God which leads us into peace.
Let us reflect your goodness and love, O Lord.
Let us pray that men and women all over the world may be healed and set free from whatever prevents them reflecting God's love, whether that springs from emotional damage, deliberate wrong choices or arrogance and hypocrisy.
Let us reflect your goodness and love, O Lord.
Let us pray that all issues and political situations working against justice may be resolved and transformed with sensitivity and wisdom.
Let us reflect your goodness and love, O Lord.
Let us pray that areas of fragile peace – in families, between tribes, and internationally – may be strengthened through needs and injustices being honestly addressed, and the cries of the voiceless being heard.

Let us reflect your goodness and love, O Lord.
Let us pray that there may be respect for one another across the boundaries of age, race and culture, so that diversity is celebrated and community is planet-wide.
Let us reflect your goodness and love, O Lord.

Our Father . . .

The great Holy Spirit of God is here among us.
God's presence fills the earth and the heavens.
As we leave this place of peace, the God of peace travels with us.
We travel in the peace and power of the living God, Father, Son and Holy Spirit.
Amen.

Under the sky

Lie on the ground with your heads at the centre and feet pointing outwards, like a clock or a star. You can relax and look up at the sky.
Choose a dry day, if possible when there is some cloud in the sky.

Here we lie, flat on the ground, with our backs against our planet home, gravity firmly strapping us on. Looking out, away from this earth, we are looking not up, but deep into the space of the solar family to which we belong: the sun, our family star, and our brother and sister planets orbiting with us and sharing our cosmic dust. We are part of the family: Mercury, Venus, Earth, Mars, Jupiter, Saturn, Uranus, Neptune and little Pluto, the furthest from the sun, our central star.
As members of this solar family, in one small part of the universe, taking up so little space on the face of just one planet, in humility we honour you, the God of truth. All things come from you, and we ourselves are part of this creation.
Glory to God, who is unseen Spirit, and full Reality; the Permanent One, giving the gift of existence to all this temporary and changing matter.
May God's radiant holiness, invisible to our physical eyes yet sensed with the God-placed spirit within us, be praised and honoured, worshipped and adored, here and in all places and times; in the heaven-lit, fragile, temporary dimension of matter, and the ordered, generous, permanent dimension of heaven.
It is through you, the great and humble God, that we have minds free to think and hearts free to love.

It is through you, the great and humble God, that we have hands for doing good and feet for bringing the good news of peace to every conflict.
Let us gaze not only into physical distance, but also into the heavenly, to marvel at both the majesty and power of God, and also at his great humility in choosing to be born as a baby in Jesus Christ.

Keep silence

Feel the planet at your back and the force pinning your body to earth.
Look deep into the distant skies.
Notice the different levels and textures of our surrounding clouds.
Look through the cloud gaps to wider distances, filled with invisible stars and planets.
Don't look directly at the sun but be aware of its shining presence.
Know that God is familiar with all you can and cannot see.
Place your trust in the One who has placed the gift of life in you.

Hymn *Holy, holy, holy is the Lord; All heaven declares* or *Immortal, invisible.*

Reading Isaiah 51:12-16; Matthew 11:25-30 or Luke 24:33-49.

This is the word of the Lord.
Thanks be to God.

'Let the same mind be in you that was in Christ Jesus:
who, though he was in the form of God, did not regard equality with God as something to be exploited,
but emptied himself, taking the form of a slave, being born in human likeness.
And being found in human form, he humbled himself and became obedient to the point of death – even death on a cross.' (Philippians 2:5-8)

Lying here under the sky we are brought face to face with the grandeur and greatness of creation, and we realise the humility of God, laying aside his majesty to make himself nothing out of love for us.
Made in the likeness of God, may we learn humility at the feet of Jesus.
As God's kingdom grows in us, we learn to long for less of self and more of God,
and discover that in serving God we are set free to live life in abundance.

Our Father . . .

Let us never forget that we live in a created world.
We pledge ourselves to look after the earth with care and humility.
As we take the time to look up into the sky surrounding our planet,
may our spiritual eyes be open to the deep reality of heaven, and the quiet, loving presence of God.
Amen.

Round a fire

Evening or night time is best for this.
It might be part of a church camp, BBQ or summer festival.
It might be a way of celebrating Jesus on the day of Hallowe'en, or at New Year.
Ensure safety at all times.
Use a fire-pit or fire basket or make a safe fireplace.
Take utmost care and arrange for everyone to be seated for the worship,
at a safe distance around the fire.

Be praised, my Lord, in brother Fire, who is so masterful and bright.
Let the power and beauty of fire remind us of the warm and loving heart of God.
As fire has so often been used as a sign of God's presence,
so may we, seated around this fire tonight, sense God's presence in all its mastery and brightness, its mystery and joy.

Hymn Sing out your praise to God in the *Clap hands Gloria; Colours of day* or *Shine, Jesus, shine.*

In the wilderness, as the people of Israel escaped from slavery in Egypt, God reassured them of his presence by a pillar of cloud going before them during the day and a pillar of fire by night.
May the fire and cloudy pillar lead us all our journey through.
Round their camp fires, the people of Israel told the stories of God's love and faithfully handed them on from generation to generation.
We thank God for those who passed the good news on to us.

Fire from heaven fell and burnt up the sacrifice to God when Elijah challenged the prophets of Baal.
May we have the courage to challenge evil and speak out for justice and peace.
It was as tongues of flame that the Holy Spirit came at Pentecost.
May we be enflamed with the fire of God's love.

Keep silence

Sit, quiet and still, round the fire.
Know that God is here with you.
As the fire brightens and warms, remember how God's love warms and brightens your hearts and lives.
In your imagination, bring into the warmth of God's love and compassion those whose lives are bleak and cold.
Allow God to set your own heart on fire with love and compassion.

Reading Daniel 3:13-28; Joel 2:28-32 or Acts 2:1-4.

This is the word of the Lord.
Thanks be to God.

May we reject the darkness of evil and selfishness and daily turn towards the light and warmth of God.
Come, Holy Spirit, take charge of my mind.
May we recognise the corruption and deceit of evil and be strengthened to resist temptation.
Lead us not into temptation but deliver us from evil.
May God's love, burning in our lives, bring hope and blessing to others.
Come, Holy Spirit, give us hearts of compassion to reach out in love.
May God burn away in our hearts anything which blocks us from his love.
Lord, I believe; help my unbelief.

Our Father . . .

Lord Jesus, who had compassion for the people because they were like sheep without a shepherd, train us as your disciples so that we may join you in working for the coming of the kingdom of heaven on earth.
Let every word we speak and every step we take be to the glory of God. May we be instruments of peace and reconciliation. May our lives shine with good works so that people see the shining and glorify God.
Let us go from here to love and serve the Lord.
In the power of God's love, we will.

On sand, mudflats or causeway at low tide

Take great care with the tide times!
Only venture out as the tide goes out.
Only stay out on the seabed for the hour of complete low tide.
Use marked paths or causeways.
Carry out a risk assessment and check the route beforehand.
Wear appropriate clothing and footwear.
Gather at the beach as the walk out together is part of the worship.

As we prepare to walk out over the sand and mud, let us pray together.
Lord God of all creation, we have come here under the wide sky to worship you.
We walk this pilgrimage out from the beach in the name of the Father, who has created the land and sea, who created the moon which has heaped up the water and drawn it away from this beach.
We walk this pilgrimage in the name of the Son of God – Jesus our Saviour – whose footprints on this earth we follow.
We walk this pilgrimage in the name of the great Holy Spirit, whose quiet wisdom and love breathes life into us and guides us into truth.
We walk this pilgrimage in the name of the blessed Three in One – Father, Son and Holy Spirit. Amen.
In our lives, we step out in faith into the unknown, and the journey is a journey of discovery.
On this pilgrimage, we step out of our comfort zone and take risks that we might not usually take. May this journeying remind us of our

calling to step out of our comfort zones and to be ready to discover more and more about the God who led his people through the sea on dry ground, out of slavery and into the wilderness on their way to the promised land.
Watch over us on this pilgrimage, O God, and as we practise our calling to look out for one another's needs, take us by the hand and lead us to a place of holiness and wonder.
Amen.

Keep silence

Walk out together on to the seabed.
Remember that where you are walking
is often completely covered with deep water.
Marvel at the watery planet we inhabit, and the ebb and flow of the tides.
Appreciate our vulnerability and the necessity of respecting God's laws of cause and effect, both physically here and also spiritually in our lives.
Stop in a suitable place to stand still and know that God is God.

Standing in the middle of the seabed, we worship the God who is hidden from our eyes but reveals himself to us spiritually, as the floor of the sea is shown to us now.
When next we look out over the full tide, we will know this place in a new and deeper way.

Reading Exodus 14:15-22; Joshua 3:5-17 or Psalm 40:1-5.

This is the word of the Lord.
Thanks be to God.

Let us pray for any who find themselves in an insecure place emotionally, mentally or spiritually; for those who are in a time of great change or turmoil in their lives.
Give them the comfort, guidance and peace of your presence, O God.

Let us pray for any who feel overwhelmed with the flood of expectations or demands on their time, resources or energy; for those who are stressed or exhausted.
Surround them with love and reassurance, O God, together with practical help in working towards a more sustainable way of living.
Let us pray for any areas which suffer from flood or drought; for our planet with its delicate balance on which we need to tread lightly and with footprints of healing, rather than damage.
Give us your wisdom and gentleness in all our living, O God.

Our Father . . .

As we walk back to the shore, let us sing with the whole of creation in praise of the God who loved all this into being.
Alleluia! Amen!

Hymn *We are marching; O, O, O how good is the Lord* or *He's got the whole world in his hands.*

In the high street

Meet at one end of the high street and the worship will take you through to the other end. This is a prayer walk, to pray for those who live and work in this town, city or village.
Choose a place to worship where you are not in anyone's way.
You are not trying to take over the place but simply to pray for it.

Peace be to this place.
Amen.
As we begin our walk, let us praise God who knows us better than we know ourselves, and loves us.

O Lord, you have searched me and known me.
You know when I sit down and when I rise up; you discern my thoughts from far away.
You search out my path and my lying down, and are acquainted with all my ways.
Such knowledge is too wonderful for me; it is so high that I cannot attain it. (From Psalm 139)

Remembering God's knowledge of us all, his concern for all creation, and his love for all who live and work here, we commit ourselves to pray for this street and this town. We thank God for all that is good and positive and bring to God's healing love any tensions or local concerns.

Hymn *Amazing grace; Be still for the presence of the Lord* or *Dear Lord and Father.*

Keep silence

Walk down the street, slowly and in silence, in twos and threes.
In your spirit, follow where Jesus walks, and pray for whomever and whatever he shows you.

Let God's vision open your eyes to all that is good and valuable.
Stop to gather where the leader stops, halfway down.

We pray for all who live and work here; for the members of the local council, for the emergency services and all who serve the community. We pray for those who teach and those who learn; for those who have businesses here and those who come to do their shopping.
God bless them and keep them.
We pray for those who have lived here in past generations and those who will live here in the future; for all who volunteer in this community; for all carers, doctors and nurses and those who are in hospital or housebound.
God bless them and keep them.
We pray for the babies and toddlers and their families; for the children and young people, and the adults – those in the prime of life and those who have lived many years.
God bless them and keep them.
We pray for any local concerns here, for any tensions or worries. We pray that all voices may be heard with genuine listening, and decisions made for the common good.
Lord, hear this prayer.
Pour out your blessing on this street today and every day.

Our Father . . .

Reading Zechariah 8:4, 5; Luke 6:46-49 or Acts 5:12-31.

This is the word of the Lord.
Thanks be to God.

Keep silence

Continue walking and praying in silence to where you have agreed to finish the walk.
Gather here.

Blessed be the Lord who daily bears us up;
God is our salvation. (Psalm 68:19)
Steadfast love and faithfulness will meet;
righteousness and peace will kiss each other.
Faithfulness will spring up from the ground,
and righteousness will look down from the sky.
(Psalm 85:11)
For the Lord is good; his steadfast love endures forever,
and his faithfulness to all generations.
(Psalm 100:5)

On an island

This may be an island you have walked out to at low tide, or reached by boat.
It may be more of a rock outcrop in a river, or it may be a fully inhabited island with ferries sailing to it.
Carry out a risk assessment and ensure that you know the tide times.
Plan your time at the island to fit in with when it is safe to be there.
Do not take any foolish risks. Ensure safety for everyone.
Choose a time when the island will not be too crowded.

We have taken the trouble to travel here, to this island to worship God. Welcome, pilgrims!
The journey here has been an important part of our worship. Just like our life's journey, we have been travelling to our destination in God's company.
We have travelled hopefully and set out in faith.
We have met with people and places, challenges and surprises.
God has guided, protected and fed us on our way.
And now we gather in a place that is surrounded by water, to learn from nature something more of the nature of God and our calling as disciples.

Keep silence

Sit in stillness, or walk around slowly.
Experience being in a place which is separate from the mainland.
Jesus often used to go off and pray in a remote place.
Let this separation make you more aware of being in God's presence.

Sometimes we need to cut ourselves off from all the demands and activity of our lives to discover the deep peace of God's Spirit within and all around us.
Sometimes we find the deep centre of meaning by moving away from all the distractions which seem so central in importance.
Lay up for yourselves treasure in heaven,
for where your treasure is, there will your heart be also.

Hymn *Seek ye first; When I look into your holiness* or *To be in your presence.*

Many saints have chosen to spend time frequently in prayer on an island, away from distractions, so as to attend to the business of God and abandon themselves to God's agenda.
Thank you, holy and merciful God, for the way you work within us and transform us.
Just as we are surrounded by water here,
so are we always surrounded by God's love.

Let us listen, with hearts as well as ears, to these words of Jesus, teaching his disciples about God's love.

Reading Mark 10:35-45; Luke 13:10-17 or John 15:8-17.

This is the word of the Lord.
Thanks be to God

While we are here, let us use some time together to pray with Jesus' heart of love for all others of the household of faith. We pray for any who need some spiritual space so they can dwell in the word of God, giving it time to take root in their lives.
Your word is a lamp to our feet.
For all who are on pilgrimage or retreat today, that God's Spirit may enfold them and draw them deeper into the heart of truth and love.

Seek first the kingdom of God and his righteousness.
For those who have recently and hesitantly started to pray, that they may discover the full beauty of holiness, the living reality of God. May there be faithful people to mentor them and friends to encourage them.
Fear not, little flock, it is the Father's good pleasure to give you the kingdom.
For those struggling to grasp what kind of being God is. For those disillusioned by the unchristian behaviour they see in Christians, and the evils, which God loathes, committed in God's name.
I am the Way, the Truth and the Life. You are the salt of the earth.

Our Father . . .

We leave this place quiet and refreshed, knowing that God is with us.

At a zoo, farm or outside pet service

Gather in a place where you are with some animals.
Ensure everyone's safety.
Make sure you are not in anyone's way.

Welcome to this holy place on the good earth and under the sky.
The earth is the Lord's and everything in it.
Let us praise God who made the heavens and the earth and all creatures.
Holy, holy, holy, Lord God almighty. Heaven and earth are full of your glory!

Praise the Lord from the earth, you sea monsters and all deeps,
mountains and all hills, fruit trees and all cedars!
Wild animals and all cattle, creeping things and flying birds!
Kings of the earth and all peoples, princes and all rulers of the earth!
Young men and women alike, old and young together! Let them praise the name of the Lord.
O praise the name of the Lord. Alleluia!
(From Psalm 148)

Reading Genesis 2:19-24; Job 38:39–39:1-4 or Luke 19:28-40.

This is the word of the Lord.
Thanks be to God.

All the creatures, plants, planets and stars are our brothers and sisters, because we are all here through our loving Maker, who is the Parent of us all.
May we look after our brothers and sisters with godly love and respect. May we not take them for granted or exploit them. May there be no

cruel treatment of them. May we live together in this universe wisely and in humility, recognising that we are all important to one another and to God.

Hymn *Let there be love shared among us*; *The Lord's my shepherd* or *He's got the whole world* – with appropriate made-up verses.

Let us give thanks to God for particular creatures we love and respect.

Give space for people to voice their own prayers of thankfulness for their favourite animals or pets.
After each person's prayer, everyone says 'Amen'.

And now let's pray for the worries we have about our planet home and the creatures we share it with.

Give space for people to voice their own prayers of concern.
After each person's prayer, everyone says 'Amen'.

Our Father . . .

Blessing of the animals.
This is a time of quiet prayer.
for each animal and those who look after them.
If you are on a farm or at a zoo, you may have everyone walking around the animals at this time of blessing.
If you are at a Pet Service, stay seated as each creature is given God's blessing.

Thank you, Lord God of all creation, for your presence here with us all today. As we go from here, may we live out our thankfulness in kind and thoughtful lives, and have the courage to do everything we can to look after our planet home.
With the help of God, we will.
Amen.

In a field, meadow or open green space

Make this the start of a picnic or BBQ, or maybe as part of a camping trip.
Dress for the weather.
Bring a few bread rolls wrapped in a cloth and arrange with a parent for a child to offer this when asked.
Sit in a circle in a place where you feel a good sense of space.
This service is suitable for families with young children.

As we settle ourselves in this wide green space under the wide sky, we honour God who made it all, including us. Let's praise him together.
Three cheers for God! Hip, hip, Hooray! Hip, hip, Hooray! Hip, hip, Hooray!

Hymn *Jesus' love is very wonderful; Give me joy in my heart* or *Praise, my soul, the King of heaven.*
Have instruments or flags available.

Jesus spent a lot of time outside. He often ate outdoors and worshipped God outdoors as we are doing now. Let's look up at the amazing sky God has made and thank him for the clouds, all of space, the distant stars and planets, our Milky Way galaxy and all the other galaxies, as we say 'Thank you, Lord God, for the sky and space and everything in it.'
Thank you, Lord God, for the sky and space and everything in it.
One day, Jesus and well over five thousand people had a picnic on a grassy place like this, under the sky. Let's look down now, at the green grass, and pick a blade of grass to look at more closely. No wonder it's called a blade!

Children: **What about under the grass?**
Under the grass are roots and ants, moles and worms, mud, pipes, layers and layers of rock, and underneath all that there's red-hot molten rock, and underneath that is the magnetic compressed core of our planet, as hot as the surface of the sun. Let's thank God for the grass, the ground, and everything deep under our feet.
Thank you, Lord God, for the grass, the ground and everything deep under our feet.
Let's hear about that picnic Jesus had with a great crowd of people.

Reading Matthew 14:13-21; Mark 6:30-44 or Luke 9:10-17.

This is the word of the Lord.
Thanks be to God.

As we imagine being there, with the disciples telling us all to sit down like this on the grass, let's do what Jesus did and share some bread together.
Who has the loaves of bread?

The child who has the bread brings it out to the leader.

Thank you for sharing this bread! Now what did Jesus do? First he thanked God for the food, so let's do that.
Thank you, God, for giving us food to keep us alive and make us strong. Thank you for the good earth where the food grows and for the people who cook meals for us. Amen.
Then Jesus started breaking the bread into small pieces and filled a basket, so let's do that.

The leader and a child assistant break the loaves into small pieces. The pieces of bread are put into a basket.

Then the disciples offered the bread to the people sitting on the grass. So let's do that.

Another person is invited to offer the bread around the group, and everyone eats. Gather up any bread left over so that nothing is wasted.

Jesus made sure there was enough for everyone before they all went home. We are going to eat our picnic in a minute, so we will be all be satisfied. God is kind and generous, and loves us to be kind and generous too.
Just before we eat our picnic, let's pray as Jesus taught his friends to pray.

Our Father . . .

As we eat our food, on our grass carpet, under our sky ceiling, we thank you, God, for looking after us so carefully and for loving us so much.
Amen.

Other Susan Sayers titles:

Patterns for Daily Prayer
1501269

Reflective Services
40 quiet and gentle acts
of worship
1501252